W9-BJH-836

DISCARDED

920
GRA

Grant, Neil

Heroes of World War II

1135

$18.60

DATE			
OCT 23 1992			
NOV 30			
DEC 07 1992			
DEC 4 1992			
MAR 23 1993			

920
GRA

HATHAWAY HIGH SCHOOL

Heroes of W

1135

BAKER & TAYLOR BOOKS

□ HEROES OF WORLD WAR II □

Fighter pilots had a glamorous image but poor odds on survival.

TALES OF COURAGE

HEROES OF WORLD WAR II

BY NEIL GRANT

Illustrated by Francis Phillipps

HATHAWAY HIGH

STECK-VAUGHN
LIBRAR
A Division of Steck-Vaughn Com
Austin, Texas

920
GRA

HATHAWAY HIGH SCHOOL

Heroes of World War II

1135

Published in the United States in 1990 by
Steck-Vaughn Co., Austin, Texas,
a subsidiary of National Education Corporation.

A Cherrytree Book

Designed and produced by
A S Publishing

Copyright © Cherrytree Press Ltd 1989

Picture credits: p2, p7 Peter Newark's Military
Pictures; p9, p13, p31, p42 Robert Hunt Library;
p10, p21, p37 (right) Topham Picture Library;
p26, p27 The Military Gallery, Universal
Promotions Ltd; p28 BBC Hulton Picture
Library; p37 (left) Anne Frank Stichting,
Amsterdam; p38 Keystone Press Agency Ltd.

All rights reserved. No part of this publication may be
reproduced, stored in a retrieval system, or transmitted, in
any form or by any means without the prior permission in
writing of the publisher, nor be otherwise circulated in any
form of binding or cover other than that in which it is
published and without a similar condition including this
condition being imposed on the subsequent purchaser.

Library of Congress Cataloging-In-Publication Data

Grant, Neil.
    Heroes of World War II/by Neil Grant: illustrated by Francis Phillipps.
        p.   cm. — (Tales of courage)
    Summary: Presents instances of heroism on both sides in World War II.
    ISBN 0-8114-2754-4
    1. World War. 1939–1945—Biography—Juvenile literature.
    [1. World War. 1939–1945—Biography.]   I. Phillipps, Francis, III.   II. Title.   III. Title:
Heroes of World War 2.   IV. Title: Heroes of World War Two.   V. Series.
    D736.G598   1990
    940.53′092′2—dc20
    [B]
    [920]   90-9468
                                                                      CIP
                                                                      AC

Printed in Italy by New Interlitho
Bound in the United States
1 2 3 4 5 6 7 8 9 0 IL 94 93 92 91 90

□ CONTENTS □

□ WORLD WAR II □

World War II began in 1939, just 20 years after World War I ended. The Germans had been defeated in the first war and were made to sign a peace treaty that treated them harshly. They believed they had been dealt with unfairly. They fostered feelings of anger.

In 1933 Adolf Hitler came to power. He told the Germans they were a "master race," who deserved to rule Europe. They would be strong again, he swore, and they would be revenged on their enemies. To Hitler, nearly everybody was an enemy – the French, Russians, Poles, and most of all, the Jews, even German Jews who were just as "German" as he was. Hitler and the Nazi Party used ruthless tactics, including the extermination of millions of innocent people.

Although Hitler was the most infamous, he was not the only brutal dictator of the 1930s. It was a troubled time in the Western world, and some people were ready to follow any leader who raised their spirits by tough talk. Hitler had an ally in the fascist, extremely right-wing dictator of Italy, Benito Mussolini. Spain, too, was ruled by a fascist dictator, although Spain, unlike Italy, took no part in the war.

The Soviet Union was also headed by a ruthless dictator. Joseph Stalin represented communism, and to fascists like Hitler and Mussolini, communism was, of course, the principal theoretical enemy. However, just before the war began, Hitler and Stalin signed an agreement that their countries would not fight each other. Hitler signed many agreements of various types. He kept his promises only as long as it suited him. When the time was ripe, he attacked the Soviet Union, agreement or no agreement.

That was later. When the war began in 1939, the Soviet Union remained neutral, in fact, it helped Germany. Hitler's chief opponents in Europe were the only large, democratic countries left – Great Britain and France.

The Germans invade

The German forces were well trained, well armed, and well supported. They were by far the best military force in Europe. With frightening speed the German tanks, followed by the German infantry and supported by the German air force, conquered Europe. When France was forced to surrender in June 1940, Hitler had no more enemies on the continent. Every country was either neutral or had been conquered.

The governments of the conquered countries had been forced to surrender, but their people had not – many fought on. Some escaped to Great Britain, others fought secretly in the resistance movement, trying to free their country from German rule. Some of the greatest heroes and heroines of the war were the Resistance fighters of occupied Europe.

The only opponent left was Britain, supported by its empire, which included Canada and Australia. The Germans could not march into Britain as they had marched into other countries because the English Channel was in the way. Hitler knew he could not launch an invasion by

American troops encountered relentless opposition in the Pacific. The Japanese defended each island to the death.

sea until the Luftwaffe (German air force) controlled the skies. But in the Battle of Britain, the Germans failed to destroy the Royal Air Force (RAF), and the invasion of Britain had to be called off.

The war also went on at sea. Britain depended on supplies from overseas, especially from North America. The German navy, using many submarines, tried to sink the ships in the Atlantic.

The turning point

In 1941 Britain was not far from defeat. Then two important events changed the situation. First, the Germans invaded the Soviet Union. As in other European countries, their initial attack was successful. But the plan was too ambitious. Even if they had conquered the whole of the huge Soviet Union, they would have needed vast armies to hold it. And

meanwhile, the Russian campaign was soaking up large quantities of German weapons, supplies, money – and men.

Even more important was that the United States entered the war on Britain's side, after the Japanese attacked the United States fleet in Pearl Harbor on December 7, 1941. The Japanese were allies of the German and Italian fascists. Their leaders, like Hitler, had convinced the people that they were some kind of master race, superior to other peoples. They, too, got results by violence and brutality. For the Japanese leaders, no less than the Nazis, justice counted for nothing, power for everything.

From 1942 to 1945 there were really two wars going on. One was the war in Europe, and North Africa, where Britain and the United States led the war against Hitler's Nazi empire. The other was the war in the Pacific and the Far East, where the United States led the fighting against the Japanese.

Once the United States entered the war, with its huge resources in money and materials, only one result was possible: the eventual defeat of the Axis powers (Germany, Japan, and Italy).

Ending the war

Germany suffered its first serious defeats in 1942. In North Africa, the Germans had come to help the Italians against the British. General Montgomery defeated them at last in a great tank battle at El Alamein. The "desert war" was over. The Germans were forced out of North Africa, and in 1943 American and British forces pursued them into Sicily, an island off the coast of southern Italy. The Italians deposed Mussolini and surrendered to the Allies. But the Germans were still in Italy, and they fought on.

The other German defeat of 1942 took place in the Soviet Union. The German army, which had been attacking the Soviet city of Stalingrad, was cut off by the Russians and forced to surrender. Six months later, another great tank battle took place at Kursk, and again the Germans were the losers.

In the Pacific, the Japanese were also slowly forced onto the defensive. They suffered terrible losses in the sea battle of Midway in 1942, and on land the U.S. Marines began to recapture islands that the Japanese had taken. Here was some of the fiercest fighting of the war. For unyielding courage, the Japanese were outstanding. As they began to lose the war in the Pacific, they took to using suicide planes. The planes were packed with explosives, and the pilots, known as *kamikaze*, dove straight into U.S. ships.

These desperate measures did not work. Island by island, the U.S. Marines advanced, while the British and Australians also advanced from India to push the Japanese conquerors out of Burma.

The Allies closed in on Germany itself. On April 30, 1945, with the Russians only half a mile away from his Berlin hideout, Hitler shot and killed himself. Four days later, the rest of the German government surrendered.

In the Far East the Japanese fought on. The fighting was cruel and ferocious, and in order to force the Japanese to surrender, the United States used a terrible new weapon — the atomic bomb. The cities of Hiroshima and Nagasaki were destroyed. Few people survived in either city, for if they were not killed by the blast, they developed cancer caused by radiation and died later. It is the only time nuclear weapons have been used in war. The atomic bombs caused the Japanese to surrender, on August 14, 1945, almost six years after the war had begun.

Heroes, sung and unsung

The war had involved everybody, not only those who did the fighting. Thousands of ordinary people were killed in cities many miles from a battlefield. Thousands were killed by armies marching through their country. Millions more were killed in death camps.

The war demanded many kinds of

courage from many kinds of people. Imagine a young woman, her husband away in the army or perhaps killed, who is trying to keep her small children alive in a city where there is little food or shelter, and the bombs descend night after night. Or imagine a Japanese *kamikaze* pilot, his plane loaded with explosives, flying straight at an American warship, knowing that he will be the first to die.

Secret wars

Another kind of courage was needed by millions of people who fought a deadly, secret war in the midst of the enemy. Resistance or "underground" fighters (Partisans) in occupied countries and spies knew that at any moment they might be arrested, tortured, and shot.

Thousands of people in many countries risked their own lives to help others.

In countries like Denmark or the Netherlands, many Jews escaped death at the hands of the Nazis only because they were protected, hidden away, by non-Jewish friends and neighbors.

Volunteers

Many people volunteered for dangerous work, not only as underground workers or spies, but as fire wardens, coast guards, in the rescue services, or doing any number of jobs that were necessary but, in wartime, dangerous. Doctors and nurses, and other medical workers, often worked in the most terrible conditions. Many died along with their patients. They, too, were heroes.

Partisans surrender to German soldiers. The partisans were usually short of food, sleep, and weapons, but not short of courage.

Winston Churchill, the "British bulldog," was an inspiring war leader.

The fighters

Among the soldiers, sailors, and airmen who fought there were many heroes on both sides. It would be possible to make a list of all the Allied fighting men who won medals like the Medal of Honor, which is awarded only for acts of greatest heroism. But, as any medal recipient will tell you, the heroes of any war are not just the ones who win the medals. In battle, and on the home front, too, some of the bravest acts and many of the most gallant people go unrecognized. They leave no record, no memory, perhaps not even a gravestone.

In battle, too, there are many kinds of heroes. The person who gets a medal, who makes headlines in the newspapers, is the kind of hero we think of first. He or she is the soldier who charges a machine-gun post single-handed, or the one who sticks to his or her post when already dying of wounds. He or she is the person who performs one amazing act of supreme heroism.

Old soldiers will claim that this kind of bravery is actually quite common. For most people it is harder to find the courage to face danger every day, for weeks on end, often in horrid places and with not enough food or sleep.

Fighter pilots are often portrayed as having had a wonderful time. They earned a reputation in many countries for being high-spirited. Yet more realistically the fighter pilot knew that he would probably be killed within a couple of weeks, or a month *if he was lucky*.

Submariners knew their lives were likely to be short. And the end, when it came for them, would be especially terrifying, imprisoned in a large metal tube far beneath the surface of the sea.

The agony of command

Besides the fighting men themselves, their commanders, whether heroic or not, certainly needed plenty of courage. In World War II good fighting generals were just as likely to be killed or wounded as the men they led, but that was only to be expected. Few generals lost much sleep over that risk. But generals plan battles and campaigns: they know that their decisions will result in the death of hundreds of their own men, and they know that if they make the wrong decision the dead will number thousands. It was a general, after all, who said, long ago, that "War is Hell."

□ BLITZ □

The German word *blitzkrieg* means "lightning war." It described the devastating German method of swift attack, using tanks and dive bombers.

In the summer of 1940, the Germans began their air attack on Britain. At first the German bombers concentrated on airfields, hoping to put the RAF out of action. When this failed, they changed the target. From September on they began to bomb British cities, especially London. Londoners called this nine-month air attack the Blitz.

East London suffered most, as the German bombers tried to destroy the docks. The district of Bermondsey was one of the hardest hit. The City of London, the ancient heart of the capital, was largely destroyed, much of it in one terrible raid on December 29, 1940.

The bombers came by day and, especially, by night. Hundreds of ordinary men and women were killed or injured. Their homes and the places where they worked were destroyed. Living conditions were terrible. Often there was no water or electricity, or even no roof!

Keeping their spirits up

Yet people remained extraordinarily cheerful. To this day, older people remember "the spirit of the Blitz," when everyone helped his or her neighbors, amid the howl and screech of falling bombs. In the most terrible situations people managed a smile, even a joke.

The king and queen, who stayed in Buckingham Palace in the middle of London during the Blitz, helped to keep people's spirits up, and so did Winston Churchill, the prime minister, who never for a moment let anyone think that Britain would not win the war.

Most of all, people kept each other's spirits up. One old woman in a house blasted by a bomb was quite annoyed when an air-raid warden arrived to help. "Get away, young man," she said, "Can't you see I'm dressing?"

Two other old women were found in the wreckage of their house holding a thermos bottle of tea. They were also cross. The bomb, they complained, had broken their teacups!

Beginning on November 2, East London was attacked for 57 nights in a row, without a break. Besides all the other horrors, it was impossible to get a decent night's sleep.

Fire bombs and land mines

In some raids most of the bombs were incendiaries – designed to start fires. From a high place London seemed a mass of bonfires. It was beautiful in a way, providing you saw it from a distance.

Every night extraordinary events were reported. There was a baby rescued from a bombed building after three days, still alive. A group of people were trapped in the cellar of a pub that collapsed about them and caught fire. They all escaped unharmed.

A few nights later the Labour Institute in Bermondsey was destroyed by a land mine. Land mines were worse than bombs because they came down slowly on a parachute and exploded on the surface. Bombs, coming down fast, usually penetrated the ground so that the surrounding buildings did not receive the full force of the explosion.

Many bombs did not explode. They lay in the rubble, a terrifying threat, until brave men trained for the job came to put them out of action.

In the ruins of the Labour Institute rescuers found a man standing on a pool table but completely buried. They got his head and shoulders free when a wall, which was still standing but unsupported by anything, suddenly collapsed on top of them. Two of the rescuers made a "human bridge" over the trapped man until he could be pulled clear. In spite of their brave action, the man died, and the two rescuers were badly injured.

When a high-explosive bomb penetrated an air-raid shelter at London Bridge underground station, the heavy steel doors were hurled inward and the water main burst. Many people were crushed by the doors or drowned by the water. A doctor and two nurses lost their lives trying to help the injured.

Sometimes the raids lasted twelve hours or more. Sometimes the bombs were incendiaries, sometimes high-explosive, sometimes land mines, sometimes all three together. On one terrible night, a bomb burst among people sheltering in a railroad arch. Rescuers had to work in horrible conditions. People who were still alive had to be pulled from a mass of dismembered bodies. Chunks fell off the bridge as they worked to free the survivors and fire blazed from a broken gas main. That bomb killed 77 people and injured many more.

Death and devastation

The injuries were not only injuries to the body. Such terrible experiences affect people's minds too, sometimes permanently.

Dealing with the dead bodies was a huge problem. Finding shelter for the homeless was even worse. In the middle of the Blitz, about 25,000 people in London were homeless. Outside London air raids were not as concentrated. Coventry suffered from one dreadful raid that killed over 500 people and destroyed the cathedral, among other buildings. Altogether, 60,000 people in Britain were killed in air raids, and about 250,000 were injured – many crippled for life.

The bombing of Germany

For the people of large German cities, the bombing was even worse. On two nights in July 1943, British bombers almost destroyed the old port of Hamburg with 10,000 tons of explosives. Over 70,000 civilians died in Hamburg altogether. In February 1945, when Germany was almost defeated, most of the beautiful city of Dresden disappeared in a gigantic firestorm caused by bombs. About 35,000 men, women, and children were burned to death. At this same time, advancing Russian troops were murdering unknown numbers of Germans in revenge for the Nazi murders in the Soviet Union. The German people had no money, no food, no safe water, and no hope. They paid a heavy price for the mad ambition of their leaders.

A scene from the London Blitz. In earlier wars, only members of the armed forces had to display "bravery under fire." In World War II, civilians had to, as well.

□ AUSCHWITZ VOLUNTEER □

When the Nazis conquered Poland in 1939, the Polish army ceased to exist. Many Polish soldiers joined the "underground" army. Witold Pilecki was one of them.

German rule in occupied Poland was even more vicious than it was in other occupied countries, and the Poles were brave resisters. There are thousands of stories about brave Poles like Witold Pilecki. Pilecki wanted to go to the prison camp at Auschwitz, where many of his fellow countrymen had been sent. His plan was to start a resistance movement among the prisoners.

It wasn't difficult. The Gestapo (secret police) were continuously arresting people in Warsaw, the Polish capital, for no reason. Pilecki simply got himself arrested. He was carrying a forged identity card, with a false name. If the Gestapo had found out who he was, he would have been shot. They didn't find out, but they knew his identity card was forged, so they sent him to Auschwitz — at that time just a camp for political prisoners.

Inside Auschwitz

The Nazi system brought out the worst in people. The Germans who ran the prison camp were cruel because they thought it was perfectly all right to treat Poles like dangerous animals. Prisoners were tortured and shot for the slightest reason, or for no reason.

Pilecki wanted to raise the prisoners' spirits, to give them courage to help each other and defend themselves if the Nazis decided to destroy the camp. He organized his helpers into groups of five. Outside their own group, no one knew anything of the others, so they could not give the other groups away even if they were tortured.

Pilecki set up groups in different parts of the camp. The hospital was one important place in Pilecki's system. The German guards usually kept away from it to avoid catching some dreadful disease. If prisoners became seriously ill, they simply shot them.

With his chosen men running the hospital, Pilecki was able to save many lives. He also controlled other parts of the camp, like the work office that organized the jobs that the prisoners were forced to do. He kept in contact with the Underground outside the camp by smuggling out messages in wooden statues which were carved by some prisoners for sale in local markets. Some of his reports eventually reached England and were broadcast by radio to occupied Europe.

After a year or two, Pilecki began to organize his resistance workers into military units, able to fight the Germans if it became necessary. But he needed weapons for them. The situation was urgent, for Auschwitz had just been changed into a death camp for Polish Jews. Huge ovens were built to burn the bodies of those who were murdered.

Leaving the death camp

Pilecki decided he must get out. He had been at work inside the camp for three years, and it was a miracle he had not been discovered already. His organization was now very large, and sooner or later he was bound to be caught. So he planned an escape.

With ordinary suits under their prison uniforms, Pilecki and two friends planned to get out through the prison bakery, for which they had a handmade key. A doctor among the prisoners had made a chemical that would destroy their scent, so the German police dogs could not track them.

They got out of the camp without being seen, and had almost reached the nearby river when they heard the alarm sounding. The river was wide and the current strong, too strong for swimming. There was a boat, but it was chained up and padlocked.

By great good luck, Pilecki discovered that the key that had opened the bakery door also opened the padlock! A few days later they were among friends in the Warsaw Underground. To Pilecki's distress, he was told there were no weapons to spare for the prisoners in Auschwitz. There was nothing more he could do.

Auschwitz continued to operate until near the end of the war, when the Germans hurriedly closed it down and destroyed the records. But such a huge crime against the human race cannot be so easily hidden. One of those who gave evidence at the trials of the criminals of Auschwitz and other death camps after the war was Witold Pilecki.

Although, amazingly, he had survived the war, Pilecki did not live much longer. After the Germans had been driven out of Poland, the Russians moved in. Pilecki continued to fight for a free Poland. He was caught by the Russians and shot in 1948.

Pilecki's plan works, as the Gestapo check his identity card. They know it is a fake, but they never found out that Pilecki was a member of the Underground.

THE *JERVIS BAY*

The *Jervis Bay* was a sheepdog, trying to bring her flock home safely. The *Admiral Scheer* was a raider, which hunted helpless merchant ships like a wolf hunting sheep.

On November 5, 1940, Captain Edward Fogarty Fegen was in command of the *Jervis Bay*. His job was to protect a convoy of 38 merchant ships, which were bringing food, oil, and other badly needed supplies across the Atlantic to Britain.

The *Jervis Bay* was not much of a warship. Before the war it had been a liner, not a very modern one either. It had been converted, and given seven six-inch (152-mm) guns, as a convoy escort. Most of the crew were merchant seamen, who had never been in a battle.

Another warship was sailing in the same part of the Atlantic that day. It was the German pocket-battleship *Admiral Scheer*. A pocket-battleship was smaller than a normal battleship, but faster, and with equally powerful guns.

In the afternoon, about the time when the sailors on the *Jervis Bay* were drinking their mugs of tea, the ship was sighted on the horizon. Captain Fegen stared at it through his binoculars. "Enemy raider!" he snapped. "Action stations!"

He ordered the convoy to scatter, put on speed, and make smoke (making a smokescreen to hide them from view). The *Admiral Scheer* had already seen the convoy and turned toward it. As the ships scattered, putting on speed and gushing out thick blankets of heavy smoke, the German captain had to pick one of them as his first target.

Before he had a chance to sink one of the helpless merchant ships, the *Jervis Bay* also changed course and put on speed. But instead of running for cover, it steamed straight at the *Admiral Scheer*.

Drawing fire

As everyone on board knew, the *Jervis Bay* had no chance. The *Admiral Scheer* had six 11-inch (28-mm) guns with a range far longer than the guns of the *Jervis Bay*. But Captain Fegen's job was to protect the ships, at all costs. And while the *Admiral Scheer* was fighting him, it could not chase the convoy.

The *Admiral Scheer* opened fire on the *Jervis Bay* and, after one or two near misses, a shell exploded near the bridge. Captain Fegen was badly wounded, with one arm almost blown off. But he stayed in command of his ship, as the German raider poured in its deadly fire.

The *Jervis Bay* was shooting back as it came within range, and it did score one hit. But by this time the ship was in terrible trouble. It was on fire, had taken a hit below the water line, and was beginning to list. Then a shot hit the engine room and brought it to a complete stop. Captain Fegen gave the order to abandon ship.

Only one lifeboat was still undamaged, and as it was lowered to the water a stray shot made a hole in it. There were still the life rafts, and the sailors climbed onto them. The Germans kept up their fire, although it was obvious that the *Jervis Bay* was sinking.

Still blazing, the gallant old ship slipped slowly under the water, stern first. Looking back, the crew could see their captain still at his place on the bridge, covered in blood and near death.

As the *Jervis Bay* sank, the *Admiral Scheer* turned away at last to chase the merchantmen. Nearly three hours had passed since it had come in sight of them. The *Jervis Bay*'s brave fight had given the convoy such a lead that nearly every ship reached a British port safely.

Saving the survivors

One of the convoy, a Swedish ship commanded by Sven Olander, had been near enough to see the *Jervis Bay* go down. As it sank, leaving the sailors, most of them wounded, drifting in the middle of the ocean, Captain Olander called his crew together. He asked them to make a choice. Should they put on full speed and get away from the danger area? Or should they go back and pick up the survivors of the crew of the *Jervis Bay*? Everyone voted to go back.

The crew of the *Jervis Bay* were landed in Canada some time later, except for those who died in the battle. Among the dead was the captain, who had gone down with his ship. His bravery was recognized by the posthumous (after death) award of the Victoria Cross.

The Jervis Bay *goes down in a blaze of fire – and a blaze of glory – while the* Admiral Scheer *heads after the merchant ships.*

□ HUMAN TORPEDO □

Being a submariner demanded courage. You had to be a real hero to ride a torpedo into enemy waters.

Ordinary submarines could rove the oceans without being spotted, but they could not hide so easily near land. They certainly could not sail right into an enemy harbor. But midget submarines could!

Although the British were fighting a losing battle in the Atlantic, in the Mediterranean the Royal Navy still ruled the waves. Admiral Cunningham, the British commander-in-chief in his base at Alexandria, Egypt's chief port, could feel satisfied. The Italian navy was no match for him.

Pigs of war

But the Italians had a secret weapon. They called it a pig! It was really no more than a kind of torpedo, though it traveled more slowly than a real torpedo, and had two seats fitted to it. It could travel for short distances on the surface or underwater, with the two-man crew breathing through oxygen masks.

On December 15, 1941, the Italian submarine *Scirè* set a course for Alexandria. It carried three "pigs" and their crews (six men), led by an officer named De la Penne.

The *Scirè* arrived off Alexandria soon after dark on December 20 and launched the three pigs. The British were about to get an early and unwanted Christmas present!

Inside the harbor were two British battleships, the *Queen Elizabeth*, with Admiral Cunningham on board, and the *Valiant*, and other, smaller ships.

Harbors were protected against submarines by underwater metal nets. But midget submarines could usually penetrate them. As it happened, the net at Alexandria was not in place, and the three pigs sailed straight through.

Each pig chose its target. De la Penne made for the *Valiant*. As they drew near, De la Penne's partner was swept off his seat. He managed to swim to a buoy while De la Penne continued on his own. He carried a mine with 650 pounds of explosives to fix to the ship's hull. But two men were needed to fix it, so he had to leave the mine on the harbor bottom, a short distance below the ship. It was set to explode in several hours' time.

Then, according to plan, he sank his pig. It did not have enough power to get back to the *Scirè*, which, for safety's sake, had moved farther away. He joined his partner on the buoy, and they were soon spotted and taken prisoner by the British. Although they said nothing, the British could guess what they had been up to. It was not the first time they had come across these Italian pig riders!

Waiting politely

The British scraped the bottom of the *Valiant* with a cable, but found nothing. However, Admiral Cunningham ordered that the two Italians should be held on board the *Valiant* in a place *below the waterline*. If the ship was blown up, they would be the first casualties.

The prisoners sat it out. After some time, De la Penne asked to speak to Captain Morgan, who commanded the *Valiant*.

"Captain," he said politely, "your ship is going to blow up in exactly five minutes!" He had waited until it was too late to save the ship but not to save lives. No one was badly hurt when the explosion came, but the *Valiant* was ripped open. Four minutes later, there was another tremendous explosion on the *Queen Elizabeth*. Admiral Cunningham was thrown into the air. A third explosion blew a hole in a tanker and badly damaged a destroyer moored next to it.

The six Italian pig pilots spent the rest

The "pig" riders found the underwater nets were not in place at Alexandria.

of the war in a British prisoner-of-war camp. But that had been expected, and their work in Alexandria harbor had been worth it. Six very brave men had put two battleships and a destroyer out of action in one night. For a short time at least, the British had lost command of the Mediterranean.

At the end of the war, De la Penne was awarded the Medaglio d'Oro, the highest award given in Italy. The man who pinned the medal to his uniform was Vice Admiral Morgan, who had been captain of the *Valiant* on the night of the raid.

□ MALTA GC □

Bombed continuously, the little island of Malta defended itself with "a heroism and devotion that will long be famous in history."

The George Cross is the medal for bravery in Great Britain that is awarded to civilians. Several rescue workers and firemen won it in the Blitz. It was once awarded, not to one person, but to a whole nation – the Maltese. It was King George VI who spoke of the islanders' heroism and devotion.

In 1942 the Germans and their Italian allies decided that they must capture the island of Malta. This would give them control of the shipping routes across the Mediterranean.

Before invading the island, which would not be easy, they planned to smash it to pieces first. They gathered a force of more than 1,000 aircraft in Sicily for this purpose.

Because the Germans commanded the air, it was very difficult to get any help or supplies into Malta. Supplies could be brought in only at great risk, either by sea or by air. In February a convoy that tried to reach Malta was completely destroyed – every ship sunk. Later, a squadron of Spitfire fighters, brought in to fight the bombers, was completely destroyed before the planes could take off again.

A few fast, single ships did get through, and some submarines. Otherwise the islanders would have starved. Food was in terribly short supply. Beans cost a penny each, and all food was strictly rationed. The Maltese had only about half as much food as Londoners in the Blitz. As if any more bad luck was needed, it was a cold and wet winter.

Merciless bombing

The bombers pounded Malta day and night. People were forced to spend most of their time living in shelters underground. Even in the deepest shelters they could feel the earth shuddering. The din was terrific. One Maltese, who was a boy during the siege, remembered people being thrown on top of each other, screaming children, diving planes, whistling bombs, huge explosions, and the bang-bang-bang of the guns that never stopped.

In the month of January 1942, there were 262 air raids on Malta. In February there were 236, and in March 275. The Germans had learned the value of not letting the defenders get rest or sleep.

The towns and villages of Malta were soon in ruins. The houses, built of heavy stone blocks, collapsed in heaps like toy bricks. Some areas were cut off for days by piles of rubble. The lavatories and sewers were broken; the smell was horrible, and disease broke out. The beautiful blue Grand Harbor of Malta turned into a dark, oily lake filled with shipwrecks.

It seemed impossible for Malta to survive. In June, two convoys were sent with supplies, one from the east and one from the west. Every ship in the eastern convoy was sunk. From the western convoy, which started out with 17 ships, only two managed to reach the island.

Saved at last

Yet Malta held out, and in the end it was saved by events in North Africa. The defeat of the Germans there changed the whole position in the Mediterranean area. The Germans lost command of the air and were forced to retreat. The next convoy that reached Malta did not lose a single ship. The siege was over.

Malta is smaller in area than Greater London. Yet nearly twice as many bombs fell on Malta in 1942 as fell on London. In Malta, the "blitz" lasted longer, and food rations were smaller.

The constant crash and thump of the bombs and the answering guns, which had gone on for months on end, made people's minds go numb. Nothing much seemed to matter anymore except looking after the family and staying alive for one more day. After the war, when Maltese people were asked about the siege, many of them could remember very little about it. They didn't mind talking about it, it was just that they had nothing to say. Time had somehow got lost.

Above: The island of Malta, a proud but battered citadel in the Mediterranean, after months of continual bombing.
Below: In a rare quiet moment, people examine the wreckage of their homes.

21

□ SPY □

In constant fear of detection, the spy leads a dangerous double life every hour in the day, every day in the week, and every month in the year.

All the governments and armies in World War II tried to get secret information about their enemies, and all used spies to get it for them.

If a soldier or airman was captured and thought a spy by the enemy, he or she was sure to be tortured, then shot or hanged. No mercy was shown to spies.

Most spies *were* caught sooner or later, so spies had to be people of great courage – that quiet, tough kind of courage that keeps a person going day after day. As for being a hero, that depended on whose side the spy was on.

Reporting for whom?

Probably the most skillful, most successful spy in World War II was Richard Sorge. Sorge was a German newspaper reporter. In 1933, he was sent to report from Tokyo, capital of Japan. The warlike Japanese had recently attacked China and taken a large slice of its land. The question people were asking was: Which way would the Japanese attack next? Would they strike north, against the Soviet Union? Or south, against the rich island nations of the Pacific?

As a newsman, Sorge was naturally interested in finding the answer to this

Through his diplomatic connections, Sorge met some of the top men in Japan at receptions like this at the German embassy.

question. But he had a stronger reason than that. For Sorge was also a secret agent of the Soviet Union, who had been trained as a spy in Moscow. He had already been a spy for the Russians in other countries, including Britain. In Tokyo, he would be more valuable.

Sorge was a loyal communist. He did not become a spy for money, but because he believed that communism, the system of the Soviet Union, was right.

Sorge was very clever, very experienced, and very brave. Although the Japanese were suspicious of him, as they were of all foreigners, he was able to build up a spy ring in Japan. It included Hotsumi Ozaki, a Japanese newspaperman who knew important men in government, Yotoku Miyagi, who knew some high-up army officers, and Max Klausen, another German, who was a businessman in Tokyo.

Friends in high places

Sorge himself became friendly with the German ambassador in Tokyo, so friendly that the ambassador let him use a room in the German embassy as an office. Thus Sorge was able to spy on his own country, Germany, as well as Japan. He was so well trusted that he was told the secret code in which messages were sent between Berlin and the Tokyo embassy.

Sorge spied for the Soviet Union in Tokyo for nine years, and sent much valuable information to Moscow. If it was a short message, he sent it by radio. But radio transmitters could be tracked down, so more often he sent his material by messengers, who were passing through Tokyo on innocent business.

The Japanese knew there was a spy ring at work in Tokyo. They had listened to some of Sorge's radio transmissions. But they could not understand the code he used, and they could not track down his transmitter.

Information supplied to order

Through his contacts in the German embassy, Sorge discovered that the Nazis were planning to attack Russia in 1941. He even discovered the date – June 22. The Russians did not dream that Hitler would break the treaty he had signed promising not to attack them, and they simply did not believe Sorge's warning. They put his message in a file for "Doubtful Information," and the German invasion took them completely by surprise. But that was not Sorge's fault.

It was now even more important to find out if the Japanese were planning to attack the Soviet Union, or if they planned to attack in the south instead. Sorge collected all the clues he could, and eventually he found out that the Japanese were definitely *not* planning to attack the Soviets. He radioed the news to Moscow in great excitement.

A spy's reward

The main job of the Sorge spy ring was now over. As things turned out, Sorge's work had been completed in the nick of time. Soon afterward, one of his agents was arrested by the Japanese secret police. This led to the discovery of the whole ring. Sorge was arrested. He and Ozaki were hanged. Miyagi died in prison from the effects of torture. Klausen survived. He was put in prison and released at the end of the war.

In the Soviet Union today, Sorge is regarded as a great hero. In Germany and Japan, of course, he is not.

□ THE REPORTER □

The best of the war reporters told the people at home what the war was really like on the battlefield. It was cruel, dirty, and unfair. Ernie Pyle was the best.

Everywhere that armies went in World War II, reporters went, too. There was no television then. Newspaper and radio reporters were all-important. The reporters were mostly a little older than the soldiers, but they lived alongside them. They ate the same food and slept in the same uncomfortable places. They even wore a soldier's uniform. But instead of a gun, they carried a pencil and notepad. Ernie Pyle was a young newspaper reporter in the United States when war broke out in Europe.

Ernie wanted to get a job as a war reporter so badly, he told a friend, that he would explode if he did not get it. He was married by this time and his wife did not want him to go, but in the end Ernie got his way.

From sideline to frontline
Ernie arrived in England just in time to report the Blitz. At first, he felt like a tourist at the war. It was still an adventure, and he did not feel personally involved. His own country was not yet in the war.

Life near the front line, he wrote, was simpler than life at home. There were only four things that the men worried about – clothes, food, cigarettes, and trying not to get shot. They did not dream about being heroes, and the one thing they really looked forward to was getting the war over so they could go home.

Spending a day watching men kill and being killed, Ernie Pyle wrote in a letter home, was "like a living nightmare." There were times when he felt he would have to get away from the war before it drove him mad. Now he was involved! The Americans were involved, too.

In the limelight
Ernie reported the long American campaign in North Africa, and he was with the American forces when they invaded Sicily. After that campaign, he went home for a while and found that his articles had made him famous. They were being printed together as a book, and a film was to be made from the book. The author was awarded the Pulitzer prize, the top prize for American writers, and as well as being famous, he was growing rich. He could very easily stay at home now and bask in his wealth and glory.

But in spite of fame and money (and in spite of the illness of his wife), he soon returned to the war. He was more and more afraid of being shot, but he had become closely attached to the ordinary soldiers. He felt a sense of duty toward them. It was up to him, he believed, to make Americans back home, who were safe, warm, and comfortable, understand just how much the soldiers suffered for their sake. What the soldiers suffered, Ernie Pyle suffered, too.

He had some narrow escapes. Once, the house he was sleeping in was blown up, and everyone thought he had been killed. But a few minutes later he clambered out of the ruins with nothing worse than a cut face. In Normandy, after the Allies invaded France, he again had a feeling that he would be killed, and he nearly was when American planes bombed their own soldiers by mistake.

Certain to be killed

When the war in Europe was coming to an end, Ernie Pyle left for the Pacific, where the Americans were fighting the Japanese. In between he had a few weeks at home. It was a hectic time. Everyone wanted to see him, and he was rushed from place to place. He was glad, he wrote, to get back to "normal routine." By "normal routine" he meant the war!

When the U.S. Marines invaded Okinawa, Ernie Pyle was with them. Even more certain he would be killed, he swore that this would be the last landing he would make with attacking troops.

After two days, he went back to the ship to write his articles.

A few days later the Marines invaded another Japanese island. True to his promise, Ernie Pyle did not go with them but waited until the next day, when the immediate fighting was over, before he went ashore. He was traveling in a jeep with some soldiers, looking for a good place to set up the command post, when a Japanese sniper opened fire from his hiding place. Ernie Pyle was shot in the head and killed at once.

His last war report was found in his pocket after his death. It was about what would happen when the war was over. The living would rejoice, Ernie wrote, and rightly so, but they should not forget the dead — those who had given their lives to buy victory and peace.

Ernie Pyle died as he may have wished, killed instantly in action.

□ DAM BUSTERS □

During the Battle of Britain, only the Royal Air Force's fighter pilots (the famous "Few," as Winston Churchill named them) stood between Britain and defeat.

Many of the most famous British heroes of World War II were pilots in the Royal Air Force. It is, of course, easier to make a pilot into a hero than an ordinary soldier. He is one man in his airplane against the enemy. It was a bit like being a medieval knight on his war horse.

Fighters and bombers
One of the most famous of these champions of the air was Douglas Bader, who lost both legs in an airplane crash before the war began. In spite of having no legs, he became a great fighter leader during the Battle of Britain, and his wooden legs were an advantage when he collided with a German fighter over France. As he tried to bail out of his crashing Spitfire, his foot became trapped inside the cockpit. But because it was not a real foot, he came to no harm when it was wrenched off.

He was taken prisoner, and later the RAF dropped a new leg by parachute, which the Germans delivered to Bader. They came to wish they hadn't, for in spite of his wooden legs Bader made many attempts to escape. Finally, the Germans sent him to Colditz Castle, a prison for especially dangerous escapees.

Among bomber pilots, two of the finest were Leonard Cheshire and Guy Gibson. Both at different times commanded

The "dam busters" performed one of the most dangerous flying feats of the war — at heavy cost in men and airplanes.

27

the RAF's most famous bomber squadron, 617 Squadron. Like Bader, Cheshire survived the war and afterward he became a worker for charity, especially for the disabled. He created the Cheshire Homes for physically handicapped people, which exist today in about 30 countries.

□ GUY GIBSON □

Guy Gibson was everyone's idea of what an RAF pilot should be – cheerful, full of fun, and completely fearless. He became a pilot two years before the war and took part in the first British bombing raid.

Aircrews were supposed to take a rest after they had flown on a certain number of raids. Guy Gibson's idea of a rest from being a bomber pilot was to fly night fighters for a spell instead. Then it was back to bombers and the command of 617 Squadron.

The night on which Gibson won his Victoria Cross, the highest British award for gallantry in war, was the night of the dam busters.

The purpose of this unusual bombing raid was to destroy three big dams in the main industrial region of Germany, the Ruhr. This was easier said than done. Not only were the dams heavily defended by searchlights and anti-aircraft guns, the bombs would have to be dropped in exactly the right spot. Ordinary bombing would not be accurate enough.

The "bouncing bomb"
The inventor Barnes Wallis solved the problem with his "bouncing bomb." Completely round like a ball, it was dropped onto the surface of the reservoir behind the dam, and skipped along the

The war over, Douglas Bader chats with Lord Dowding, who led the fighter command to victory in the Battle of Britain.

top of the water until it reached the dam. Then it sank to the bottom and exploded, blowing a hole in the base of the dam.

The bombers had to fly in very low, at night, over water, keeping a steady course, while the German guns blazed all around them. Gibson made the first run and, when he had dropped his bomb, he flew back and forth to draw the gunfire toward his own plane and away from those making their bombing runs. It was for this courageous act that he gained his VC.

Surprisingly, Gibson returned safely from the dam busters' raid. But 53 men did not. When Barnes Wallis heard how many had been killed, he blamed himself. "If I'd known, I'd never have started this business," he said. The dams *were* broken, though German industry was not harmed as badly as the British had hoped.

Guy Gibson went on to fly in many more raids. But in September 1944 his plane caught fire and crashed in Holland, and he was killed.

□ BRINGING RELIEF □

Even in total war, some people try to limit the effects of its cruelty by looking after civilians, prisoners of war, the wounded, and others who cannot help themselves.

The Red Cross (Red Crescent in Muslim countries) is the main international relief organization. During World War II the Red Cross tried to keep records of all prisoners of war and civilians in prison camps. It made more than 11,000 visits to such camps. It supplied clothing and medical supplies (it even had its own fleet of 12 ships), and it tried to persuade the warring countries to obey international rules of war.

There were just as many heroes and heroines to be found in the Red Cross and in other relief organizations (including the churches) as there were among the armies, navies, and air forces. One of them was Teresa Nava.

□ SAVING THE CHILDREN □

In 1945 the tide of war in the Pacific had turned against the Japanese. The Americans were advancing steadily. But the Japanese still held Manila, the capital city of the Philippines.

Teresa Nava had 39 children left in her care in a Manila children's home. Things had been bad for a long time, but by this stage almost every normal part of life had broken down. Nothing was working.

Teresa had just enough rice, gruel, and fish to feed her children two more meals.

After that they would go hungry, unless she could reach Red Cross headquarters for more supplies. Yet to move in the streets of Manila was deadly dangerous. She would become a target for a sniper's bullet the moment she stepped outside. What should she do?

The next day her question was answered for her. A shell tore away the front of the house where the children were, and they had to move. Teresa marched them out of the back and over the fence. They had gone only a few yards when another shell blast destroyed what was left of their home.

For three days the tired and hungry children straggled through the back streets, dodging the shells and taking cover where they could.

Places to shelter became fewer, and food was nowhere to be had. The only refuge, it seemed to Teresa, was the General Hospital. But that was on the other side of the main street, which the Japanese still controlled. They fired on any human figure who appeared on it.

In desperation, Teresa made herself a red cross flag from a piece of red cloth and a pillowcase. She pinned it to a cane and, mustering all her courage, she started out on her deadly journey.

The Japanese were so astonished, or impressed, by the figure of the lone woman with her homemade Red Cross flag that they did not fire. In fact, they bowed their heads in respect while Teresa ferried every one of her children across that terrible road, and so brought them to safety in the General Hospital.

□ THE PARTISANS □

Underground resistance movements evolved in the occupied countries. In the Soviet Union the Germans were never safe from Partisan guerrilla fighters and saboteurs.

When the Germans invaded the Soviet Union in 1941, they advanced with great speed toward Moscow. The Soviet defenders were swept aside. The Russian armies were quickly defeated, but the Russian people were not. Behind the German lines, the Partisans were soon at work.

The Partisans were ordinary people, including many young women, who formed secret bands in the forests and villages to resist the invaders. Some of the bands were started by soldiers who had been cut off from their comrades by the advancing Germans. Their purpose was to make difficulties for Germans wherever they could, cutting telephone lines, blowing up bridges and railroad lines, setting fire to stores and supplies, and laying traps.

To begin with they had very few weapons or supplies. The lack of medical supplies, even bandages, meant that nothing could be done to help the wounded. Many died from wounds that would have been easy to treat in normal times. Others died of cold and hunger.

Many stories are told in the Soviet Union of the bravery of the Partisans. Thousands and thousands of ordinary Russian people acted with the greatest courage against the enemies of their country. Thousands lost their lives. If those people had lived to tell their stories, we should have many, many more accounts of the heroes of the Soviet Union.

Nazi terror

The Nazis despised the Russians. They considered them a second-rate nation. They were as ready to kill them as they were to kill rats. The Nazis ruled by terror. Sometimes they killed every person in a village, including children, because someone in the village had given food to the Partisans. They rounded up young people in the towns and sent them off to Germany to work as slaves.

In one district where the Partisans had been especially active, the Germans burned down 158 villages. All the men from those villages were sent away to the German slave-labor camps. All the women, children, and old people were murdered in cold blood.

This behavior made even more Russians join the Partisans.

The Partisans blew up hundreds of trains and killed thousands of Germans — exactly how many, no one knows. One high Nazi official had a beautiful Russian girlfriend, or he thought she was his girlfriend. But he was blown up by a bomb under his bed soon after he met her.

Partisans who were captured could expect no mercy. They could not even expect a quick death. The Germans were so enraged by the damage the Partisans were doing to them that they tortured them horribly before they killed them.

▫ Zoya ▫

Although this happened to thousands of Russians, one name is well known. It is the name of Zoya Kosmodemianskaya, a symbol of the Partisans. Zoya was sent behind the German lines on a secret mission. But, soon after setting fire to a German stable, she was captured in the village of Petrishchevo, near Moscow. The Germans tortured her and then hanged her in the village square, forcing the people to watch her die. She was 18 years old.

Zoya is remembered only by chance.

It happened that a reporter of the Soviet newspaper, *Pravda*, entered the village of Petrishchevo two weeks later, after the Germans had been driven out. Zoya's body was still hanging there by the rope around her neck, frozen stiff in the cruel Russian winter. That reporter told her story and made her name a symbol of Russian heroism. But there were many Zoyas.

Zoya Kosmodemianskaya is led to her execution. The placard around her neck lists her "crimes" against the Germans.

□ WHO WAS THAT FOOL? □

With one sudden, spectacular act of courage, a corporal accomplished what a whole company could not.

The only part of the United States that was occupied by the Japanese was a few of the Aleutian Islands, off Alaska. This was part of the Pacific War, but up near Alaska the Pacific is not so sunny and blue as it is in the south. It is gray and cold, and the islands are covered with snow. There was snow on the hill that Colonel Finn was trying to capture in the winter of 1942.

The Japanese were dug into foxholes on the top of the hill. The Americans opened fire on them with mortars (small cannons that throw bombs) and machine guns. Under cover of this heavy fire, Captain Johnson's men moved out and up the hill. The Japanese guns began to chatter, kicking up the snow around them. Two men fell, dead, before they reached the safety of a rocky ledge.

They still had 80 yards to go beyond the ledge, and there was no cover. Below them, their machine guns kept firing at the top of the hill where the Japanese were holed up.

One by one, Johnson's men began to scramble up the steep slope, slipping on the wet rock. Another man fell, and another. When they had almost reached the top, Colonel Finn ordered the machine guns to stop firing. The Japanese had stopped firing, too. For a few moments there was a deathly hush. Then the Japanese came to life. Grenades came whizzing from their foxholes, exploding among Johnson's men and sending them slithering and sliding down the slope again. Colonel Finn's machine guns opened up, trying to make the Japanese stop firing while Johnson's men started to climb back up the hill.

Once more they had almost reached the top when the grenades came flying over the ridge, driving them back down the hill. But one man clung to the top. As the gunfire died away for a moment, he pulled himself up over the ridge. He could be seen clearly from where Colonel Finn stood, across the valley. He fired his rifle into a foxhole, and then threw in a grenade. Then he moved on to the next hole, dancing back and forth and somehow dodging the bullets and bombs that whined and banged all around him. Crack! went his rifle, followed by another grenade. All the way along the ridge he went, firing his rifle, throwing his grenades, until he reached the end. At the last hole he had run out of bullets, so he jumped in swinging his rifle like a club. Climbing out, he signaled to his friends down the hill that it was safe to come up.

Colonel Finn had watched all this in disbelief. Who was that fool? It turned out to be a Corporal George Mirich, whose job was to stay at company headquarters and take messages. The colonel was never able to figure out how he'd got on that hill in the first place.

The company clerk captures the ridge! Corporal Mirich goes into action. Amazingly, he escaped with only an injured arm.

THE GURKHAS

For their fighting ferocity and courage, the Gurkhas are admired and feared. Their name has become a symbol of bravery in battle.

The Gurkhas come from Nepal and serve in the British army. They can be called mercenaries, because they fight for wages in a foreign army, but they are much more than mercenaries. They have a proud tradition of honor and loyalty, which is passed from father to son in the mountain villages of Nepal.

There was nothing unusual about Jitbahadur Rai, who led a platoon during a minor battle in Italy in 1944. Strangely, this battle was watched from a safe observation post by King George VI, although he was too far away to see how Jitbahadur Rai won his medal for gallantry.

It was Jitbahadur Rai's first battle. Not long before he had been a waiter in the officers' mess, or dining room. He and his men were pinned down by German machine-gun fire, and there was not much they could do except keep their heads down. But the bullets set fire to some dry grass, and faced only by smoke from the burning grass, the machine guns stopped for a moment.

Jitbahadur takes his chance

At once Jitbahadur Rai was up and running. His men followed. Like most Gurkhas, he was a small man, and when he reached the German machine-gun post, it was manned by two enormous German gunners. But, with two or three swipes of his kukrie, the heavy, curved knife carried by all Gurkha soldiers, he killed them both.

Unfortunately, they fell on top of him, and when a third gunner appeared, Jitbahadur Rai was unable to struggle free. His men arrived just in time to take the third gunner prisoner.

Later, Jitbahadur Rai was seen walking next to the stretcher carrying the wounded prisoner. He was still carrying his blood-stained kukrie in one hand, and patting the prisoner's shoulder with

the other. He was talking at a great rate, telling the German that he need fear nothing more now that he was a prisoner. Since Jitbahadur Rai spoke in his own language, Gurkhali, it is not likely that the German understood him!

Courage in battle

Soldiers in North Africa used to tell stories of Gurkha scouts going out at night and returning with the heads of German sentries. A British officer who served with them said, "Of one thing I am certain, it is wise to be on the same side as the Gurkhas."

And yet, in spite of all these tales of fantastic bravery, Gurkhas were really no different from other soldiers. They were tough, but they were not supermen. Many Gurkhas won VCs, the U.K.'s highest medal for bravery, and many more deserved to, but they all felt the fear of being killed or wounded, like the soldiers of any nation in any war. Courage in battle cannot be counted on. Anyone may be as brave as a lion one day and a shivering coward the next.

Jitbahadur Rai is pinned down by the two hefty machine-gunners he killed in his valiant charge through the smoke.

□ ANNE FRANK □

Anne Frank's diary, written in terrifying and constricting circumstances, is a deeply moving record of a young girl's courage.

In June 1942, Anne Frank had her 13th birthday. Her family were German Jews, who had fled to Holland when the Nazis came to power in 1933. But now the Germans had conquered Holland, and with them came their hatred of all Jews.

Anne had to wear a yellow star on her sleeve, to show she was Jewish. She had to obey all the rules made by the Nazis to make life difficult for Jews. She could not, for example, travel on a streetcar, or ride a bicycle, or stay outside after eight o'clock in the evening.

A month later, the Gestapo started rounding up the Jews in Holland. This was not unexpected, and for months Anne's father had been preparing a hiding place for his family. He owned an office building in Amsterdam that had two upper floors tucked away at the back of the building. They could be reached only by a narrow staircase, which could be hidden by moving a bookcase in front of it.

The building was looked after by two Dutchmen, who bravely and generously looked after the Frank family — Anne, her parents, and her older sister, Margot. Soon they were joined in their secret home by another family, Mr. and Mrs. van Daan with their 15-year-old son, Peter, and by a dentist named Dussel.

They all lived in the secret hideout for over two years. For every minute of every day they had to take care not to be seen or heard. During the day the rest of the building was in use, so they had to be especially careful until the workers went home at five-thirty. Imagine a lively 13-year-old sent to bed as punishment on a fine afternoon. Then imagine the punishment lasting two years.

A daily record of courage

We do not have to imagine what life was like in that hideout, because Anne kept a diary. She wrote everything in it, not only the things that happened, since not very much *could* happen, but all her thoughts and feelings. She was a born writer, and surely would have been a fine novelist if she had been allowed to grow up. By reading her diary, we get to know Anne very well.

She was a clever, kind, intelligent girl, with a gift for looking on the bright side. When you read her diary, it is easy to forget the dreadful life she was forced to lead in that attic in Amsterdam.

We have a photograph of her with her diary in front of her. She had a charming smile, something many people said of her. Once, when she told Peter van Daan she would like to help him, he replied, "You do, every day, with your gaiety."

It may seem a strange thing to say of a child, but Anne had a wonderfully strong character. Almost nothing got her down. She somehow knew that the only way to live is with joy and courage, no matter how grim life is. Some people grow old without learning that.

In June 1944, the Allies invaded

German-occupied France. Anne wrote in her diary:

> Great commotion in the Secret House! Would the long-awaited liberation that has been talked of so much, but which still seems *too* wonderful, *too* much like a fairy tale, ever come true? . . . The best part of the invasion is that I have the feeling that friends are approaching. We have been oppressed by those terrible Germans for so long, they have had their knives so at our throats, that the thought of friends and delivery fills us with confidence. . . . Perhaps, Margot says, I may yet be able to go back to school in September. . . .

But Anne never went back to school. A year's hard fighting still lay ahead for the Allied forces. Meanwhile, Anne and her family remained in their secret house.

Above: The house in which Anne Frank and her family lived their secret life for over two years.
Right: Anne photographed just before the war with her father.

Dit is een foto, zoals
ik me zou wensen,
altijd zo te zijn.
Dan had ik nog wel
een kans om naar
Holywood te komen.

Annefrank.
10 Oct. 1942

*Anne wrote the caption to this picture
herself: "This photo shows me as I would
wish myself to look all the time. Then maybe
I would have a chance to go to Hollywood."*

There was a good deal of quarreling, for people get on each other's nerves when they are cooped up together for months on end. But the dream of freedom kept them going.

The diary stops

In August 1944, the Gestapo raided the house. Everyone was arrested, including the two Dutchmen who had been taking care of them. The Jews were packed into railroad trucks meant for cattle and taken to camps in eastern Europe.

The family was separated. Anne and her sister went from one terrible death camp at Auschwitz to another at Belsen, where they lived for over six months. People who knew her there said that Anne showed the same strength and courage that had kept her lively and even happy in the secret house.

In February 1945, both girls caught the dangerous disease, typhoid. One day, as Margot tried to get up from her bunk, she fell to the floor. Because she was so weak with starvation and illness, it was enough to kill her. Anne was now alone, and she could not fight any longer. Her wonderful spirit weakened at last, and she died a few days after Margot.

Of all the Jews who had hidden in the secret house in Amsterdam, only Anne's father was still alive at the end of the war. When he got back to Amsterdam, he was given Anne's diary, which had been found in the wreckage left by the Gestapo. Now, that diary belongs to the world, and Anne Frank, who died at the age of 15, has become the symbol of the six million Jews – men, women, and children – who were murdered by the Nazis during World War II.

□ THE RESISTANCE □

At first resistance in France consisted of spontaneous acts of sabotage by individuals. Gradually the French Forces of the Interior, known as the *maquis,* became a well-organized movement.

When France surrendered in 1940, part of the country was occupied by German forces. The rest was not under German rule, but under a French government at Vichy, which obeyed the Germans.

Few French people supported the Germans. Some escaped to Britain to carry on the fight; General De Gaulle was one of them. Others stayed in France and joined the Resistance.

The British wanted to help the Resistance, because of course the Resistance was a help to them by committing acts of sabotage.

In London, SOE (Special Operations Executive) was the organization in charge of the secret war in Europe, which went on in all the occupied countries. SOE sent weapons and supplies when it could. It also sent its own agents to help organize the Resistance.

□ ODETTE □

One of these was Odette Sansom. She was a French woman who had married an Englishman and lived in England. She was 30 years old and had three young daughters when she volunteered to work for SOE.

In 1942 a fishing boat in the Mediterranean pulled into a quiet part of the French coast one night, and Odette slipped ashore. The Resistance fighters knew when she was coming, and she soon joined up with the man she was to work with – Peter Churchill, known as "Raoul." He was one of the chief British agents in southern France, and his main job was to get the different groups in the Resistance to work together, and to carry out the acts that Britain wanted. Odette, being both French and English, was an ideal assistant.

In the months that followed Odette traveled about on her secret work and was almost captured more than once. One day, she was traveling by train with a radio set in her suitcase (in those days radios were large and heavy). A German officer helped her put the case on the luggage rack. "Well, madame," he said, "your bag *is* heavy. What have you got in it, a radio set?" And they both laughed at his joke.

Another close call resulted from an attempt to fly Raoul back to London to discuss future plans with SOE. There was a small airfield, no longer in use, where the RAF could land a plane. First, Raoul and Odette went to find out if it was safe. They walked around it with their arms around each other, pretending to be lovers out for a stroll. But while they held hands and giggled, their eyes were searching for signs of danger.

Everything looked all right. The buildings seemed to be empty. Grass was growing on the runway. Thick woods grew on the other side of the airfield, and if things went wrong, they would be able

to escape that way. A message was sent to London, and a few days later London signaled the date and time on which the plane would land.

The night of the landing was cold and still. There was a little mist at ground level, but not enough to stop the plane from landing. In the shadow of the trees, Odette waited with Raoul and two other Resistance men, eating ham sandwiches and drinking brandy. In an hour or two, if all went well, Raoul would be in England.

Danger!
They heard the plane's engines, and lit the torches that marked the runway. The plane came into sight, a dark shape against the sky. At that moment lights blazed out from the airfield buildings. Shouts could be heard, and the lights went out again. But they had seen and heard enough. It was a trap!

They flashed a "danger" signal to the airplane and scattered. Odette, walking quickly, headed for the woods. When she was among the trees she stopped for a moment to watch the British airplane turning away.

It vanished and all was quiet again. Odette went on through the woods, toward the road. Then she heard a sound that made her heart turn to ice. The bark of a dog!

She knew that she could escape from

Arrest and more resistance

Odette's luck did not last forever, though. A few months later, the Gestapo, the German secret police, raided a hotel where she and Raoul were staying. They were arrested.

Odette refused to give the names of other members of her Resistance group, although she was tortured to make her talk. Her back was burned with a red-hot iron, and her toenails were pulled out with pincers. At last, the Gestapo gave up, and sent her to the women's

Odette threw the tracker dogs off her scent by plunging into a river and struggling across to the other side.

men among the trees. But a dog would follow her scent. She started running, deep into the woods. She could hear the dog behind her, getting nearer, as she raced through the trees. Once she caught her foot and fell with a crash into the undergrowth. She pulled herself up and ran on, gasping for breath. The dog was so near she could hear it panting.

Suddenly she came to the end of the woods. Just beyond was a river. What luck! Dogs can't follow a scent through water. She plunged into the freezing river and, half swimming, half wading, reached the other side. The road was close then. As she reached it, she heard a man's voice calling to the dog. She had made it!

death camp at Ravensbruck. But the Germans thought she might be an important person, because she said she was married to Raoul, who was a distant relation of the British prime minister. As their forces were by this time on the retreat, they decided that important prisoners like Odette and Raoul should be kept alive. Odette lived to tell her story. Many of SOE's agents did not.

Some of the Resistance fighter's equipment, including radio, knife, pistol, and cameras.

◻ MADELEINE ◻

One person who did not survive was Noor Inayat Khan, code-name Madeleine. Half Indian and half American, she had been to school in Paris and spoke perfect French. In peacetime she had written books for children, but in 1943 she was a radio operator for SOE in occupied Paris.

The Germans had ways of tracking down secret radio transmitters, and anyone found with one was likely to be shot. No more dangerous job existed.

Madeleine worked with a Resistance group known as PROSPER. Their job was to upset the German system as much as possible, and to inform London about the movement of German troops.

Like many other Resistance groups, PROSPER was broken up when the Gestapo arrested one of its agents. Through him they learned about many of the others, who were quickly arrested. Madeleine must have known that her days were numbered, but she refused a chance to escape to England because she was the only trained radio operator left in the Paris Resistance.

To avoid arrest, she had to keep moving all the time. She hardly ever slept in the same house two nights in a row. She always made all her broadcasts from a different place. Carrying the radio transmitter in a small suitcase, she moved around the Paris area, always looking over her shoulder, always listening for the sound of boots on the staircase.

For some time she kept one step ahead of the Gestapo. Then, one afternoon while she was sending a coded broadcast to London, the door crashed open and German soldiers burst in.

The Gestapo questioned her and, when she refused to tell them what they wanted, they beat her savagely. But she still had the strength to break away from them while she was being taken back to her cell. She did not get far.

After days of questions and torture, she was sent to a prison in Germany where she was chained in a cell so small she could not stand up or lie down in it. After nearly a year of this treatment, she was taken to the death camp at Dachau, where she was shot as a spy.

□ GERMAN RESISTERS □

Perhaps the bravest of all the "resisters" were the Germans who resisted the Nazis. "Traitors" to their fatherland, they risked their lives out of loyalty to what is right.

It took courage for men and women in occupied countries to fight against the German rulers. They were inspired by patriotism, by love of their own country, and hatred of its foreign conquerors.

The Nazi rule of Hitler made itself more hateful by being cruel and evil. For the millions of innocent people who were killed by Nazi Germany, it made no difference if their murderers were Nazis or not.

A great many Germans during World War II disliked their own government. But what could they do about it? Someone who resists a foreign conqueror is a hero. But someone who resists his or her own government is a traitor.

Germany did not have a united Resistance movement. But among many different groups of people, a few existed whose hatred of Nazism was so strong that they were ready to face almost certain death by opposing Hitler's rule.

a bold, new leader who would build a better Germany. As he came to understand the Nazis better, Hans's admiration turned to disgust, then hatred.

The White Rose students printed leaflets that attacked the evils of Nazi rule and asked people to stop supporting it. The movement spread to universities in other cities. No one knows how many students shared the beliefs of Hans and Sophie, but it was probably a very large number. On one surprising day, a high-up Nazi official gave a talk to the students, *and was loudly booed*. It is hard for us to realize what an extraordinary thing that was in Nazi Germany, when people could be arrested just for listening to a British radio broadcast.

The Scholls were arrested and executed in 1943. Their families were also arrested, because the Nazis thought a family containing one traitor might contain more. Altogether, 16 White Rose students were killed.

These students were heroically brave, but they had no chance of stopping Hitler. Nor did the clergymen and other groups who stood up and spoke out against the Nazis before the war began.

□ THE WHITE ROSE □

Two students, Hans and Sophie Scholl, led a Resistance group at the University of Munich. Their movement was known as the White Rose. Hans Scholl had once been an admirer of Hitler. Like many young Germans, he believed in Hitler as

□ KILLING HITLER □

The only people who could really do something about Hitler were the military leaders. Although some of them were true Nazis, many were not. There were plots against Hitler by close military advisers, and at least six attempts to arrest him or kill him between 1938 and 1944. Once, a bomb was smuggled on board his plane, but it failed to go off. Hitler seemed to lead a charmed life.

The last attempt, in July 1944, was nearly successful. Colonel von Stauffenberg placed a briefcase containing a bomb in a room where Hitler was holding a meeting. This time the bomb did go off, but a few minutes before, someone had moved the briefcase, and Hitler was not seriously hurt.

A terrible slaughter followed as Hitler took his revenge. Thousands were killed, including no less than 18 generals. Some were strangled to death with wire. One of those who died was Field Marshal Rommel, the best German general of the war, who was a national hero. He was advised to commit suicide: Hitler did not want a scandal over such a popular war hero. Rommel obeyed because, otherwise, he was told, his wife and child would be sent to a concentration camp. As it happened, Rommel had not taken part in the bomb plot. But he had probably known about it, and he had certainly hoped it would succeed.

Von Stauffenberg planted the briefcase and left the meeting, confident that he would soon hear "news" of Hitler's death.

□ HEROES A-Z □

Anielewicz, Mordechai (1919-1943) Leader of Jewish Combat Organization that fought the unequal battle during the Warsaw ghetto uprising in 1943.

Annand, Richard (1914-) Won first VC of the war, for conspicuous gallantry, in fighting on the Dyle Canal in Belgium in 1940, including rescuing his wounded aide, though badly wounded himself.

Aosta, Duke of (1898-1942) Governor General of Italian East Africa when the war began, he conducted a gallant campaign against the British before surrendering in May 1941. He died of tuberculosis in a prisoner-of-war camp in Kenya.

Bader, Douglas (1910-1982) Having lost both legs in a flying accident in 1931, he commanded 242 Squadron during the Battle of Britain. After colliding with a Luftwaffe fighter over France in August 1941, he bailed out and was captured.

Beurling, George (1922-1948) Canadian ace with the RAF; in 14 days of air fighting over Malta in 1942, he shot down 27 Axis aircraft.

Blakeslee, Donald (1915-) U.S. fighter ace who flew first with RAF's Eagle Squadron (133), then with USAAF's 4th Fighter Group which destroyed 1,016 enemy aircraft. He shot down 15 and destroyed two on the ground.

Bong, Richard (1920-1945) Leading U.S. ace who destroyed 40 Japanese aircraft. He was killed in a flying accident just before V-J Day.

Bonhoeffer, Dietrich (1906-1945) German Lutheran pastor and theologian who was employed during the war by the German army. A leader of the "spiritual resistance" to the Nazis, and was hanged at Flossenberg concentration camp.

Borghese, Prince Valerio (1912-1974) Italian naval commander of the assault force that disabled HMS *Queen Elizabeth* and *Valiant* in Alexandria harbor in 1941. He was awarded Italy's highest military decoration, the Gold Medal of Valour.

Bor-Komorowski, Tadeusz (1895-1966) From 1943, he led the Polish Home Army. In August 1944 he launched the Warsaw Uprising and held out for 63 days, with the loss of 250,000 Polish lives. He was imprisoned in Colditz and lived in exile after the war.

Crabb, Lionel (1910-1956?) British naval officer who served at Gibraltar as a mine and bomb disposal "frogman." His expertise helped keep Italian ports clear for Allied shipping and landing craft. He was awarded the George Medal for "gallantry and undaunted devotion to duty."

De Jongh, Andree (1916-) Belgian Resistance leader who founded the "Comet Line," an escape route for Allied POWs and shot-down airmen that rescued 800 in all. Captured by Nazis, she survived two years in a concentration camp. She was awarded the British George Medal.

Devereux, James (1903-1988) U.S. Marine officer who led heroic defense of Wake Island in December 1941. He is said to have signaled "Send us more Japs" after repelling initial attacks. He survived the rest of the war in Japanese prison camps.

Doss, Desmond (1923-) U.S. army medic with the infantry on Okinawa in May 1945. A Seventh Day Adventist and conscientious objector, he won the Medal of Honor for saving many comrades' lives, despite being wounded himself.

Esmonde, Eugene (1909-1942) Irish officer in Royal Navy's Fleet Air Arm who was awarded a posthumous VC for leading an attack on the German battle cruisers *Scharnhorst* and *Gneisenau* and cruiser *Prinz Eugen* during the "Channel Dash."

Fegen, Edward Fogarty (1895-1940) Royal Navy officer who was awarded posthumous VC for his sacrificial gallantry as commander of the armed merchant cruiser HMS *Jervis Bay* which was sunk by the German pocket-battleship *Admiral Scheer* in 1940. By taking on the *Scheer*, he enabled the convoy to escape.

Frank, Anne (1929-1945) Jewish girl whose diary has become a "poignant symbol of Jewish suffering." She, her parents, and others hid for over two years in concealed rooms above an Amsterdam office. Betrayed and arrested in 1944, Anne died in Belsen concentration camp.

Gibson, Guy (1918-1944) Leader of 617 Squadron in attack on Mohne and Eder dams in May 1943. He was awarded VC, but was killed over Holland.

Guerisse, Albert (1911-1989) Belgian doctor, code-named Pat O'Leary, who ran a secret escape organization that enabled hundreds of Allied airmen to evade capture and return to Britain. He was betrayed and sent to Dachau concentration camp where he organized the International Prisoners Committee. He was awarded the George Cross.

Hilary, Richard (1918-1943) RAF fighter and war author. He was shot down, badly burned, and maimed, but returned to active service and was killed in a flying accident.

Hollis, Stanley (1912-1962) Recipient of the only VC awarded for action on D-Day; in an assault on the Mont Fleury battery, he charged a pill box single-handed under heavy fire, cleared a trench, and saved his company from an attack.

Howard, Charles (1906-1941) British earl and bomb disposal expert, killed while attempting to defuse two bombs. He was awarded a posthumous George Cross.

Inayat Khan, Noor (1914-1945) Resistance fighter of Indian and American parentage. In the summer of 1943 she worked for SOE in France under the code name Madeleine. Betrayed to the Germans, she was sent to Dachau concentration camp and shot. She was awarded a posthumous George Cross.

Kozhedub, Ivan N. (1920-) Leading RAF fighting ace, credited with shooting down 62 German aircraft.

Kretschmer, Otto (1912-) German U-boat commanding officer who sank 375,000 tons of Allied shipping, including 3 armed merchant cruisers and a destroyer. He was captured on U99 in March 1941.

MacArthur, Douglas (1880-1964) U.S. general who was Supreme Commander of Southwest Pacific Area (1942-45).

Magennis, James (1919-) Leading Seaman who took part in a midget submarine attack on a Japanese cruiser at Singapore in 1945. He and his officer Lieutenant Ian Edward Fraser both won VCs.

McAuliffe, Anthony C. (1898-1975) Acting divisional commander of the 101st U.S. Airborne Division encircled at Bastogne. He replied to the German demand to surrender with one word: "NUTS."

Mölders, Werner (1913-1941) Leading German fighter pilot who shot down 108 Allied aircraft and received the Knight's Cross with Oak Leaves, Swords and Diamonds, Germany's highest decoration.

Moulin, Jean (1899-1943) De Gaulle's representative in France as coordinator of Resistance activities. Captured by Gestapo in Lyons in June 1943, he is thought to have been tortured to death by the notorious Klaus Barbie, "Butcher of Lyons."

Murphy, Audie (1924-1971) U.S. serviceman credited with having killed, wounded, or captured 240 enemy soldiers. He became the U.S.'s most decorated soldier with 21 medals including the Congressional Medal of Honor. After the war he played himself in the film of his exploits "To Hell and Back."

Murrow, Ed (1908-1965) CBS radio correspondent whose broadcasts from London during the Blitz aroused American sympathy and support. With U.S. entry into the war, he became a war correspondent, on one occasion flying over Berlin on a raid. He entered Buchenwald concentration camp after its liberation, making a moving broadcast on the horrors he witnessed.

Ngarimu, Moana-Nui-A-Kwia (1918-1943) Maori who led an attack on the Djebel Tabarga in Tunisia in March 1943. He won a posthumous VC.

Nicholson, James B. (1917-1945) British pilot who shot down a Messerschmitt despite being wounded and half blinded in the combat. He was the only Fighter Command pilot to win a VC during the Battle of Britain.

Osborn, John R. (1899-1941) Canadian serviceman who threw himself on a hand grenade during the defense of Hong Kong, killing himself but saving the lives of his comrades. He won a posthumous VC.

Pyle, Ernie (1900-1945) War correspondent whose accounts of American soldiers in battle won him a Pulitzer Prize in 1944. "Every GI regarded him as a friend," it was claimed. He was killed by machine-gun fire on the island of Ii-shima, near Okinawa.

Rommel, Erwin (1891-1944) German general and field marshall who commanded the Afrika Korps and earned the nickname "Desert Fox." Implicated in the plot to kill Hitler, he chose to take poison rather than be tried.

Sansom, Odette (1912-) Resistance heroine who worked with Peter Churchill's SOE network in France. She was captured and tortured by having her back seared with a red-hot iron and her toenails pulled out. She was sent to Ravensbruck concentration camp and escaped death only because the Germans believed her to be Winston Churchill's niece by marriage.

Schindler, Oskar (1908-1974) German businessman from the Sudetenland who had factories in occupied Poland. He managed to protect and save the lives of hundreds of Polish Jews from the Cracow ghetto.

Schmid, Anton (1900-1942) Wehrmacht sergeant major who helped to save Jews in the Vilna ghetto (Lithuania). Executed by the Nazis, his tombstone reads: "Here rests a man who thought it was more important to help his fellow men than to live."

Scholl, Sophie (1921-1943) Munich University student and, together with her brother **Hans (1918-1943)**, leader of the White Rose resistance group. To People's Court president Roland Feister, at her trial, she said, "You know as well as we do

MAIN EVENTS OF WORLD WAR II

1939
Germany invades Poland (Sept. 1); Britain and France declare war (Sept. 3); Russia invades Finland (Nov. 30); Battle of Plate River (Dec. 13).

1940
Germany invades Denmark and Norway (Apr. 9), then Holland, Belgium, Luxembourg, and France (May 10); Evacuation from Dunkirk (May 27-June 4); Italy declares war on Britain and France (June 10); France signs armistice with Germany (June 21); Battle of Britain (July 1-Oct. 1); Blitz on Britain (Sept. 7-May 10, 1941).

1941
Germany invades Greece and Yugoslavia (Apr. 6); Germany invades Russia (June 22); Japanese attack Pearl Harbor (Dec. 7).

1942
Fall of Singapore (Feb. 15); U.S. landings on Guadalcanal (Aug. 7); Dieppe Raid (Aug. 19); Battle of El Alamein begins (Oct. 23); Allies land in North Africa (Nov. 8); Russians open counteroffensive at Stalingrad (Nov. 19).

1943
Germans surrender at Stalingrad (Feb. 1); The Dams Raid (May 16); British and U.S. troops land in Sicily (July 10); Mussolini deposed (July 25); Italians sign armistice with Allies (Sept. 3); Salerno landing (Sept. 9); Tehran Conference (Nov. 29-Dec. 2).

1944
Anzio landing (Jan. 22); Cassino captured by Poles (May 18); Rome entered by Allies (June 4); D-Day-Allied landings in Normandy (June 6); Attempt on Hitler's life (July 20); Warsaw uprising (Aug. 1); Paris liberated (Aug. 23); Arnhem airborne attack (Sept. 17); Ardennes offensive (Dec. 16).

1945
Warsaw liberated (Jan. 17); Yalta conference (Feb. 5-12); Rhine crossed by Allies (Mar. 23); President Roosevelt dies (Apr. 12); Mussolini executed (Apr. 28); Hitler commits suicide (Apr. 30); Victory in Europe (VE) Day (May 8); First atomic bomb on Hiroshima (Aug. 6); Second atomic bomb on Nagasaki (Aug. 9); Japan surrenders (Aug. 14); Formal surrender of Japan on USS Missouri in Tokyo Bay (Sept. 2).

---

that the war is lost. Why are you so cowardly that you won't admit it?"

Stauffenberg, Claus Von (1907-1944) German army officer who carried out an almost successful assassination attempt on Hitler on July 20, 1944. He was shot the same night; his last words: "Long live our sacred Germany!"

Sukanaivalu, Sefania (?-1944) Fijian corporal who was awarded the VC for gallantry and self-sacrifice while serving in the Solomon Isles. He rescued two wounded men under fire before being hit himself while rescuing a third.

Szabo, Violette (1921-1945) Former Brixton shop worker who joined SOE's French Section after the death of her Free French officer husband. Captured by the Nazis near Limoges in June 1944, she was shot at Ravensbruck concentration camp.

Upham, Charles (1908-) New Zealander who was the only man to win a VC bar during the war. He won his first award for gallantry in the Crete campaign in 1941 and the bar for further conspicuous gallantry in the Western desert in 1942.

Wake, Nancy (1916-) Australian-born French Resistance fighter who parachuted into the Auvergne in February 1944. She planned and took part in sabotage attacks of prearranged targets on D-Day, including the German headquarters at Montlucon. Her husband had been murdered by the Gestapo in 1943.

Walker, Frederic (1896-1944) British officer described by Churchill as "our most outstanding U-boat killer." Between December 1941 and June 1942 his 36th Group destroyed 7 U-boats. He went on to command 2nd Escort Group.

Wallenberg, Raoul (1912-) Swedish diplomat in Budapest. During the summer of 1944, his courageous action saved thousands of Hungarian Jews from the gas chambers. After outwitting the Nazi mass murderer, Adolf Eichmann, he was taken into "protective custody" by the Russians. His fate remains unknown.

Werra, Franz Von (1914-1941) German fighter pilot, shot down during the Battle of Britain, who managed to escape from Canada and return to Germany via the United States and Mexico – the only man to do so. He was awarded the Knight's Cross.

Yeo-Thomas, Forest Frederick (1902-1964) Served with SOE's French section, under the code-name "White Rabbit." He made three missions to coordinate Resistance activities after Jean Moulin's arrest. Betrayed by a subordinate, he was tortured and sent to Buchenwald concentration camp, from which he escaped. He was awarded the George Cross.

□ INDEX □